MARIANNE MOORE

That Harp You Play So Well

FORGOTTEN POETS

Editor | Dick Whyte   Number 23 | 2024

MARIANNE MOORE (1887-1972) was born in Kirkwood Missouri, and attended Bryn Mawr College from 1905, where she met fellow poet Hilda Doolittle. Moore majored in history, economics, and political science, and in her spare time was involved with the suffrage movement. She also began writing short-stories and poetry, published in *Tipyn O'Bob*, the Bryn Mawr literary magazine. By 1915 she was publishing work in *The Egoist* and *Poetry*, two of the leading publishers of 'new verse'. In 1918 Moore and her mother moved to New York, and she became a part of the Greenwich Village art scene, was active in *Others* magazine, edited by Walter Conrad Arsenberg, and *Bruno's Weekly*, edited by Guido Bruno, and her work was praised by poets like Doolittle, Harriet Monroe, William Carlos Williams, and Ezra Pound. In 1921 Moore's first collection of poetry was published in England without her knowledge by partners Doolittle and Bryher. A few years later in 1924 Moore published her first official book of poetry, *Obervations*, and took up editorship for the arts magazine *The Dial*, from 1925 until 1929. After a period of seclusion, Moore achieved some fame as a poet and personality of New York when her book *Collected Poems* won the Pullizer Prize in 1951.

Publication credits: Selections from *Poems* (1921) & *Observations* (1924); with 'That Harp You Play So Well' & 'Appellate Jurisdiction' (*Poetry*, May 1915); 'To A Friend In The Making' & 'Blake' (*Others*, Dec. 1915); 'Holes Bored In a Workbag by the Scissors' & 'Apropos of Mice' (*Bruno's Weekly*, Oct. 1916); 'The Just Man And' & 'Designing A Cloak' (Dec. 1916); 'The Past Is The Present' (*Others: An Anthology*, 1917); 'Feed Me, Also, River God', 'To William Butler Yeats On Tagore', 'He Made This Screen' (*Poems*, 1921); Marriage (1923); & the essay '"New" Poetry Since 1912' (*Anthology Of Magazine Verse*, 1926), etc.

Cover: Pamela Bianco - 'The Strong Child' & 'Mirage' (*Flora*, 1919). Inside: Pamela Bianco – 'Portraits' (1919), '6 Drawings' & 'Rabbit' (*The Century*, July 1922), etc.

This collection ©2024. All individual poems and illustrations belong to the 'public domain', unless otherwise noted. Some elements of the originals may have been marginally edited, for clarity and consistency.

FORGOTTEN PRESS
Aotearoa | New Zealand

ISBN: 978-1-991310-38-5 (paperback) • 978-1-991310-39-2 (hardback)
978-1-991310-40-8 (ebook)

MARIANNE MOORE
THAT HARP YOU PLAY SO WELL

POEMS

A selection of verses from *Poems* (1921),
Observations (1924), & various magazines.

MARRIAGE

The complete poem-cycle *Marriage*,
first published 1923.

NEW VERSE

Moore's essay, *New Verse Since 1912*,
first published 1926.

FORGOTTEN POETS

edited by **Dick Whyte** .

Missing Meters! Lost Lyrics!
Vanished Verses!

FORGOTTENPOETS.COM

"Moore, using the same material as all others before her, comes at it so effectively, at a new angle, as to throw out of fashion the classical-conventional poetry to which one is used and puts her own and that about her in its place. The old stops are discarded... Furthermore there is a multiplication, a quickening, a burrowing through, a blasting aside, a dynamization, a flight over—it is 'modern', revealing the essence of poetry.

"Good modern work, far from being the fragmentary, neurotic thing its misunderstanders think it is... is a multiplication of impulses that by their several flights, crossing all eccentric angles, might enlighten. As a phase, in its slightest beginning, it is not yet nearly complete. And it is not rising as an arc: it is more a disc pierced here and there by light; distressingly broken up."

—*William Carlos Williams (1925)*

MARIANNE MOORE

P O E M S

THAT HARP YOU PLAY
SO WELL

O David, if I had
    Your power, I should be glad—
In harping, with the sling,
In patient reasoning!

Blake, Homer, Job, and you,
Have made old wine-skins new.
    Your energies have wrought
    Stout continents of thought.

But, David, if the heart
Be brass, what boots the art
    Of exorcising wrong,
    Of harping to a song?

The sceptre and the ring
And every royal thing
    Will fail. Grief's lustiness
    Must cure that harp's distress.

TO AN INTRA-MURAL RAT

You make me think of many men
    Once met to be forgot again
  Or merely resurrected
In a parenthesis of wit
That found them hastening through it
  Too brisk to be inspected.

RETICENCE
& VOLUBILITY

"When I am dead,"
     The wizard said,
  "I'll look upon the narrow way
  And this Dante,
      And know that he was right
      And he'll delight
          In my remorse,
          Of course."

  "When I am dead,"
  The student said,
      "I shall have grown so tolerant,
      I'll find I can't
          Laugh at your sorry plight
          Or take delight
          In your chagrin,
              Merlin."

APPELLATE
JURISDICTION

Fragments of sin are a part of me.
  New brooms shall sweep clean the heart of me.
  Shall they? Shall they?

When this light life shall have passed away,
God shall redeem me, a castaway.
  Shall He? Shall He?

BLAKE

I wonder if you feel as you look at us,
  As if you were seeing yourself in a mirror
      at the end
  Of a long corridor—walking frail-ly.
I am sure that we feel as we look at you,
As if we were ambiguous and all but improbable
  Reflections of the sun—shining pale-ly.

TO A FRIEND
IN THE MAKING

You wild, uncooked young fellow!
    The swinkèd hind will stumble home
    Not looking at the tasks he scorned
        to shirk.
  Impelled to respite by rough hands,
The labored ox will bellow;
      While you stand there agape before
      your handiwork.

Not all good men are mellow.
  You savor of a walnut rind,
    Of oak leaves, or plucked mullein
      on the brae.
  And yet with all your clumsiness,
You give me pleasure, fellow;
      Your candor compensates me for my
      old bouquet.

TO MILITARY PROGRESS

You use your mind
  Like a millstone to grind
  Chaff.
You polish it
And with your warped wit
  Laugh

At your torso,
Prostrate where the crow
    Falls
On such faint hearts
As its god imparts,
    Calls

And claps its wings
Till the tumult brings
    More
Black minute-men
To revive again,
    War

At little cost.
They cry for the lost
    Head
And seek their prize
Till the evening sky's
    Red.

TO A STEAM ROLLER

The illustration
  is nothing to you without the application.
    You lack half wit. You crush all the particles
      down into close conformity, and then walk
        back and forth on them.

Sparkling chips of rock
are crushed down to the level of the parent block.
    Were not "impersonal judgment in æsthetic
        matters, a metaphysical impossibility," you

might fairly achieve
it. As for butterflies, I can hardly conceive
    of one's attending upon you, but to question
        the congruence of the complement is vain,
        if it exists.

TO A CHAMELEON

Hid by the august foliage and fruit of
   the grape vine,
Twine
  Your anatomy
    Round the pruned and polished stem,
     Chameleon.
     Fire laid upon
    An emerald as long as
  The Dark King's massy
One,
Could not snap the spectrum up for food as
   you have done.

INJUDICIOUS GARDENING:
TO BROWNING

If yellow betokens infidelity,
 I am an infidel.
  I could not bear a yellow rose ill will
  Because books said that yellow boded ill,
 White promised well;

However, your particular possession—
 The sense of privacy
  In what you did—deflects from your estate
  Offending eyes, and will not tolerate
 Effrontery.

"HE WROTE THE HISTORY BOOK"

There! You shed a ray
    of whimsicality on a mask of profundity so
        terrific, that I have been dumbfounded by
it oftener than I care to say.
            The book? Titles are chaff.

Authentically
    brief and full of energy, you contribute to
            your father's
        legibility and are sufficiently
synthetic. Thank you for showing me
            your father's autograph.

DILIGENCE IS TO MAGIC
AS PROGRESS IS TO FLIGHT

With an elephant to ride upon—"with rings on
　　her fingers and bells on her toes,"
she shall outdistance calamity anywhere she goes.
Speed is not in her mind inseparable from carpets.
　　　　Locomotion arose
　　in the shape of an elephant; she clambered
　　up and chose
to travel laboriously. So far as magic carpets are
　　　　concerned, she knows
　　that although the semblance of speed may
　　attach to scarecrows
of æsthetic procedure, the substance of it is
　　　　embodied in such of those
　　tough-grained animals as have outstripped
　　man's whim to suppose
them ephemera, and have earned that fruit of
　　　　their ability to endure blows,
　　which dubs them prosaic necessities—
　　　　not curios.

TO BERNARD SHAW:
A PRIZE BIRD

You suit me well, for you can make me laugh,
Nor are you blinded by the chaff
That every wind sends spinning from the rick.

You know to think, and what you think you speak
With much of Samson's pride and bleak
Finality; and none dare bid you stop.

Pride sits you well, so strut, colossal bird.
No barnyard makes you look absurd;
Your brazen claws are staunch against defeat.

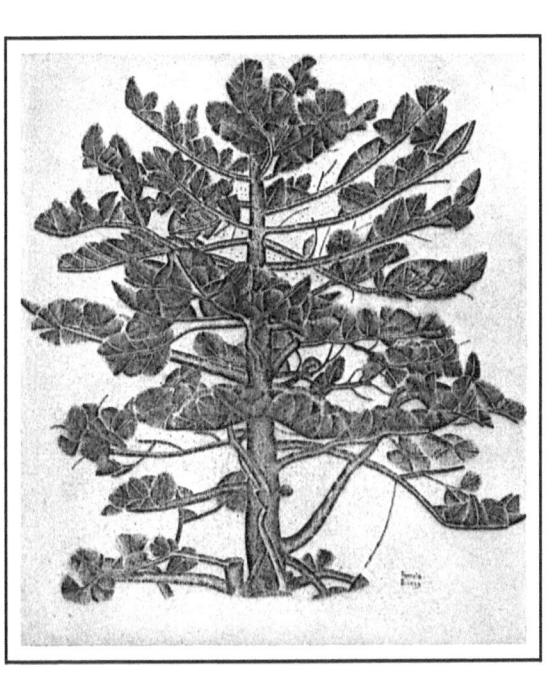

TO WILLIAM BUTLER YEATS
ON TAGORE

It is made clear by the phrase,
Even the mood—by virtue of which he says

The thing he thinks—that it pays,
To cut gems even in these conscience-less days;

But the jewel that always
Outshines ordinary jewels, is your praise.

IN "DESIGNING A CLOAK
TO CLOAK HIS DESIGNS,"
YOU WRESTLED FROM OBLIVION,
A COAT OF IMMORTALITY
FOR YOUR OWN USE

Cowed by his uningenious will
        Of dragon-like demeanor, till
    It left them orphans.
His foibles clustered underneath
Him, dominated by a wreath
        Of upright half notes.

Encumbered as he was with pride,
But for that coat he might have died
        So despicably
That kindness might have seemed unkind
Had not the garment been designed
        To serve two masters.

TO A MAN WORKING HIS
WAY THROUGH A CROWD

To Gordon Craig:

Your lynx's eye
Has found the men most fit to try
    To serve you. Ingenious creatures follow
    in your wake.

Your speech is like Ezekiel's;
You make one feel that wrath unspells
    Some mysteries—some of the cabals of
    the vision.

The most propulsive thing you say,
Is that one need not know the way,
    To be arriving. That forward smacks
    of retrospect.

Undoubtedly you overbear,
But one must do that to come where
  There is a space, a fit gymnasium for action.

HOLES BORED IN A
WORKBAG BY THE SCISSORS

A neat, round hole in the bank of the creek
    Means a rat;
    That is to say, craft, industry, resourcefulness:
      While
These indicate the unfortunate, meek
  Habitat
    Of surgery thrust home to fabricate useless
      Voids.

THE JUST MAN AND

His pie. "I would be
    Repossessed of all the
Superlatives that I have squandered,
That I might use them in praise of it."

The four and twenty
Birds were singing while he
Apportioned it off casually
And found in it nothing for himself.

APROPOS OF MICE

Come in, Rat, and eat with me;
    One must occasionally—
    If one would rate the rat at his true worth—
    Practise catholicity.

Cheeseparings and a porkrind
Stock my house—good of their kind
    But were they not, you would oblige me? Is
    Plenty, multiplicity?

TO BE LIKED BY YOU
WOULD BE A CALAMITY

"Attack is more piquant than concord," but when
  You tell me frankly that you would like to feel
My flesh beneath your feet,
   I'm all abroad; I can but put my weapon up, and
        Bow you out.
Gesticulation—it is half the language.
   Let unsheathed gesticulation be the steel
      Your courtesy must meet,
         Since in your hearing words are mute,
              which to my senses
            Are a shout.

LIKE A BULRUSH

Or the spike
of a channel marker or the
moon, he superintended the demolition of
    his image in
the water by the wind; he did not strike

them at the
time as being different from
any other inhabitant of the water;
    it was as if he
were a seal in the combined livery

of bird plus
snake; it was as if he knew that
the penguins were not fish and as if in their
    bat blindness, they did not
realize that he was amphibious.

THE PAST
IS THE PRESENT

Revived bitterness
　is unnecessary unless
　　One is ignorant.

To-morrow will be
Yesterday unless you say the
　　Days of the week back-

Ward. Last weeks' circus
Overflow frames an old grudge. Thus:
　　When you attempt to

Force the doors and come
At the cause of the shouts, you thumb
　　A brass nailed echo.

HE MADE
THIS SCREEN

Not of silver nor of coral,
But of weatherbeaten laurel.

Here, he introduced a sea
Uniform like tapestry;

Here, a fig-tree; there, a face;
There, a dragon circling space—

Designating here, a bower;
There, a pointed passion-flower.

FEED ME, ALSO,
RIVER GOD

Lest by diminished vitality and abated
    Vigilance, I become food for crocodiles—
        for that quicksand
Of gluttony which is legion. It is there—
        close at hand—
    On either side
    Of me. You remember the Israelites
        who said in pride

And stoutness of heart: "The bricks are fallen
        down, we will
Build with hewn stone, the sycamores are cut
        down, we will change to
Cedars?" I am not ambitious to dress stones,
        to renew
    Forts, nor to match
    My value in action, against their ability
        to catch

Up with arrested prosperity. I am not like
Them, indefatigable, but if you are a god you will
Not discriminate against me. Yet—
        if you may fulfill
    None but prayers dressed
    As gifts in return for your gifts—
        disregard the request.

A TALISMAN

Under a splintered mast,
   Torn from the ship and cast
      Near her hull,

A stumbling shepherd found
Embedded in the ground,
      A sea-gull

Of lapislazuli,
A scarab of the sea,
      With wings spread—

Curling its coral feet,
Parting its beak to greet
      Men long dead.

IS YOUR TOWN NINEVEH?

Why so desolate?
    in phantasmagoria about fishes,
  what disgusts you? Could
    not all personal upheaval in
      the name of freedom, be tabooed?

Is it Nineveh
  and are you Jonah
    in the sweltering east wind of your wishes?
    I myself, have stood
      there by the aquarium, looking
        at the Statue of Liberty.

FEAR IS HOPE

"No man may him hyde
From Deth holow eyed."
For us two spirits this shall not suffice,
To whom you are symbolic of a plan
Concealed within the heart of man.
Splendid with splendor hid you come,
from your Arab abode,
An incandescence smothered in the hand
of an astrologer who rode
Before you, Sun—whom you outran,
Piercing his caravan.

Sun, you shall stay
With us. Holiday
  And day of wrath shall be as one, wound
        in a device
    Of Moorish gorgeousness, round glasses spun
    To flame as hemispheres of one
      Great hourglass dwindling to a stem.

              Consume hostility;
      Employ your weapons in this meeting place
          of surging enmity.
    Insurgent feet shall not outrun
Multiplied flames, O Sun.

A FOOL, A FOUL THING,
A DISTRESSFUL LUNATIC

With webs of cool
     Chain mail and his stout heart,
          is not the gander
Mocked, and ignorantly designated yet,
To play the fool?
"Egyptian vultures clean as cherubim,
All ivory and jet," are they most foul?
And nature's child,
That most precocious water bird, the loon—why
Is he foremost in the madman's alphabet;
Why is he styled
In folly's catalogue, distressful lunatic?

AN EGYPTIAN PULLED GLASS
BOTTLE IN THE SHAPE
OF A FISH

Here we have thirst
    And patience from the first,
    And art, as in a wave held up for us to see
    In its essential perpendicularity;

Not brittle but
Intense—the spectrum, that
    Spectacular and nimble animal the fish,
    Whose scales turn aside the sun's sword
        with their polish.

ROSES ONLY

You do not seem to realise that beauty
 is a liability rather than
an asset—that in view of the fact that spirit
 creates form we are justified
 in supposing
that you must have brains. For you, a
 symbol of the unit,
 stiff and sharp,
conscious of surpassing by dint of native
 superiority and liking for everything
 self-dependent, anything an

ambitious civilisation might produce:
 for you, unaided to attempt through sheer
reserve, to confute presumptions resulting
 from observation,
 is idle.

                    You
         cannot make us
think you a delightful happen-so. But rose,
    if you are brilliant, it is not because
    your petals are the
         without-which-nothing
         of pre-eminence. You would, minus
    thorns, look like a what-is-this, a mere

peculiarity. They are not proof against
    a worm, the elements, or mildew
but what about the predatory hand? What
    is brilliance without co-ordination?
         Guarding the
    infinitesimal pieces of your mind,
         compelling audience to
the remark that it is better to be forgotten
    than to be remembered too violently,
your thorns are the best part of you.

TO A SNAIL

If "compression is the first grace of style,"
   you have it. Contractility is a virtue
as modesty is a virtue.
It is not the acquisition of any one thing
that is able to adorn,
or the incidental quality that occurs
as a concomitant of something well said,
that we value in style,
but the principle that is hid:
in the absence of feet, "a method of conclusions";
"a knowledge of principles,"
in the curious phenomenon of your occipital horn.

POETRY

I too, dislike it:
     there are things that are important
  beyond all this fiddle.

The bat, upside down; the elephant pushing,
a tireless wolf under a tree,
the base-ball fan, the statistician—
"business documents and schoolbooks"—
these phenomena are pleasing,
but when they have been fashioned
into that which is unknowable,
we are not entertained.

   It may be said of all of us
   that we do not admire what we cannot
      understand;
            enigmas are not poetry.

"THE BRICKS ARE FALLEN DOWN, WE WILL
BUILD WITH HEWN STONES. THE SYCA-
MORES ARE CUT DOWN, WE WILL
CHANGE TO CEDARS."

In what sense shall we be able to
    secure to ourselves peace and do as they did—
who, when they were not able to rid
    themselves of war, cast out fear?
    They did not say: "We shall not be brought
        into subjection by the naughtiness of the sea;
though we have 'defeated ourselves with
    false balances' and laid weapons in the scale,
glory shall spring from in-glory; hail,
    flood, earthquake, and famine shall
    not intimidate us nor shake the
        foundations of our inalienable energy."

"NOTHING WILL CURE THE SICK LION BUT TO EAT AN APE"

Perceiving that in the masked ball
attitude, there is a hollowness
that beauty's light momentum can't redeem,
  since disproportionate satisfaction anywhere
  lacks a proportionate air,

he let us know without offense
by his hands' denunciatory
upheaval, that he despised the fashion
  of curing us with an ape—making it his care
  to smother us with fresh air.

REINFORCEMENTS

The vestibule to experience is not to
be exalted into epic grandeur. These men are
going to their work with this idea, advancing
    like a school of fish through

still water—waiting to change the course or
    dismiss the idea of movement, till forced to.
        The words of the Greeks
ring in our ears, but they are vain in comparison
    with a sight like this.

The pulse of intention does not move so that one
    can see it, and moral machinery is not labelled,
but the future of time is determined
    by the power of volition.

THE PAST IS THE PRESENT

If external action is effete
    and rhyme is outmoded,
        I shall revert to you,
    Habakkuk, as on a recent occasion
            I was goaded
        into doing, by XY, who was speaking of
            unrhymed verse.
This man said—I think that I repeat
    his identical words:
        "Hebrew poetry is
prose with a sort of heightened consciousness.
            'Ecstasy affords
    the occasion and expediency determines
        the form'."

SILENCE

My father used to say,
"Superior people never make long visits,
have to be shown Longfellow's grave
nor the glass flowers at Harvard.
Self reliant like the cat—
that takes its prey to privacy,
the mouse's limp tail hanging
    like a shoelace from its mouth—
they sometimes enjoy solitude,
and can be robbed of speech
by speech which has delighted them.
The deepest feeling always shows itself
    in silence;
not in silence, but restraint."
Nor was he insincere in saying,
    "Make my house your inn."
        Inns are not residences.

MARIANNE MOORE

MARRIAGE

MARRIAGE

This institution,
        perhaps one should say enterprise
out of respect for which
one says one need not change one's mind
about a thing one has believed in,
requiring public promises
of one's intention
to fulfill a private obligation:
I wonder what Adam and Eve
think of it by this time,
this firegilt steel
alive with goldenness;
how bright it shows—
"of circular traditions and impostures,
committing many spoils,"
requiring all one's criminal ingenuity
to avoid!

Psychology which explains everything
explains nothing
and we are still in doubt.
Eve: beautiful woman—
I have seen her
when she was so handsome
she gave me a start,
able to write simultaneously
in three languages—
English, German and French
and talk in the meantime;
equally positive in demanding a commotion
and in stipulating quiet:
"I should like to be alone;"
to which the visitor replies,
"I should like to be alone;
why not be alone together?"
Below the incandescent stars
below the incandescent fruit,
the strange experience of beauty;

its existence is too much;
it tears one to pieces
and each fresh wave of consciousness
is poison.
"See her, see her in this common world,"
the central flaw
in that first crystal-fine experiment,
this amalgamation which can never be more
than an interesting impossibility,
describing it
as "that strange paradise
unlike flesh, stones,
gold or stately buildings,
the choicest piece of my life:
I am not grown up now;
I am as little as a leaf,
the heart rising
in its estate of peace
as a boat rises
with the rising of the water;"

constrained in speaking of the serpent—
shed snakeskin in the history of politeness
not to be returned to again—
that invaluable accident
exonerating Adam.
And he has beauty also;
it's distressing—the O thou
to whom from whom,
without whom nothing—Adam;
"something feline,
something colubrine"—how true!
a crouching mythological monster
in that Persian miniature of emerald mines,
raw silk—ivory white, snow white,
oyster white and six others—
that paddock full of leopards and giraffes—
long lemonyellow bodies
sown with trapezoids of blue.
Alive with words,
vibrating like a cymbal

touched before it has been struck,
he has prophesied correctly—
the industrious waterfall,
"the speedy stream
which violently bears all before it,
at one time silent as the air
and now as powerful as the wind."
"Treading chasms
on the uncertain footing of a spear,"
forgetting that there is in woman
a quality of mind
which as an instinctive manifestation
is unsafe,
he goes on speaking
in a formal customary strain,
of "past states, the present state,
seals, promises,
the evil one suffered,
the good one enjoys, hell, heaven,

everything convenient
to promote one's joy."
There is in him a state of mind
by force of which,
perceiving what it was not
intended that he should,
"he experiences a solemn Joy
in seeing that he has become an idol."
Plagued by the nightingale
in the new leaves,
with its silence
not its silence but its silences,
he says of it:
"It clothes me with a shirt of fire."
"He dares not clap his hands
to make it go on
lest it should fly off;
if he does nothing, it will sleep;
if he cries out, it will not understand."
Unnerved by the nightingale

and dazzled by the apple,
impelled by "the illusion of a fire
effectual to extinguish fire,"
compared with which
the shining of the earth
is but deformity—a fire
"as high as deep
as bright as broad
as long as life itself,"
he stumbles over marriage,
"a very trivial object indeed"
to have destroyed the attitude
in which he stood—
the ease of the philosopher
unfathered by a woman.
Unhelpful Hymen!
a kind of overgrown cupid
reduced to insignificance
by the mechanical advertising
parading as involuntary comment,

by that experiment of Adam's
with ways out but no way in—
the ritual of marriage,
augmenting all its lavishness;
its fiddic-head ferns,
lotus flowers, opuntias, white dromedaries,
its hippopotamus—
nose and mouth combined
in one magnificent hopper,
its crested screamer—
that huge bird almost a lizard,
its snake and the potent apple.
He tells us
that "for love
that will gaze an eagle blind,
that is with Hercules
climbing the trees
in the garden of the Hesperides,
from forty-five to seventy
is the best age,"

commending it
as a fine art, as an experiment,
a duty or as merely recreation.
One must not call him ruffian
nor friction a calamity—
the fight to be affectionate:
"no truth can be fully known
until it has been tried
by the tooth of disputation."
The blue panther with black eyes,
the basalt panther with blue eyes,
entirely graceful—
one must give them the path—
the black obsidian Diana
who "darkeneth her countenance
as a bear doth,"
the spiked hand
that has an affection for one
and proves it to the bone,
impatient to assure you

that impatience is the mark of independence
not of bondage.
Married people often look that way—
"seldom and cold, up and down,
mixed and malarial
with a good day and a bad."
"When do we feed?"
We occidentals are so unemotional,
we quarrel as we feed;
one's self love's labor lost,
the irony preserved
in "the Ahasuerus tête à tête banquet"
with its small orchids like snakes' tongues,
with its "good monster, lead the way,"
with little laughter
and munificence of humor
in that quixotic atmosphere of frankness
in which, "Four o'clock does not exist
but at five o'clock
the ladies in their imperious humility
are ready to receive you";

in which experience attests
that men have power
and sometimes one is made to feel it—
to make a baby scholar, not a wife.
He says, "What monarch would not blush
to have a wife
with hair like a shaving-brush?
The fact of woman
is 'not the sound of the flute
but very poison'."
She says, "Men are monopolists
of 'stars, garters, buttons
and other shining baubles'—
unfit to be the guardians
of another person's happiness."
He says, "These mummies
must be handled carefully
'the crumbs from a lion's meal,
a couple of shins and the bit of an ear',

turn to the letter M
and you will find
that 'a wife is a coffin',
that severe object
with the pleasing geometry
stipulating space not people,
refusing to be buried
and uniquely disappointing,
revengefully wrought in the attitude
of an adoring child
to a distinguished parent."
She says, "This butterfly,
this waterfly, this nomad
that has 'proposed
to settle on my hand for life'.—
What can one do with it?
There must have been more time
in Shakespeare's day
to sit and watch a play.
You know so many artists who are fools."

He says, "You know so many fools
who are not artists."
The fact forgot
that "some have merely rights
while some have obligations,"
he loves himself so much,
he can permit himself
no rival in that love.
She loves herself so much,
she cannot see herself enough
a statuette of ivory on ivory,
the logical last touch
to an expansive splendor
earned as wages for work done:
one is not rich but poor
when one can always seem so right.
What can one do for them
these savages
condemned to disaffect
all those who are not visionaries

alert to undertake the silly task
of making people noble?
This model of petrine fidelity
who "leaves her peaceful husband
only because she has seen enough of him"—
that orator reminding you,
"I am yours to command."
"Everything to do with love is mystery;
it is more than a day's work
to investigate this science."
One sees that it is rare—
that striking grasp of opposites
opposed each to the other, not to unity,
which in cycloid inclusiveness
has dwarfed the demonstration
of Columbus with the egg—
a triumph of simplicity—
that charitive Euroclydon
of frightening disinterestedness
which the world hates,
admitting:

"I am such a cow,
if I had a sorrow,
I should feel it a long time;
I am not one of those
who have a great sorrow
in the morning
and a great joy at noon;"

which says: "I have encountered it
among those unpretentious
protegés of wisdom,
where seeming to parade
as the debater and the Roman,
the statesmanship
of an archaic Daniel Webster
persists to their simplicity of temper
as the essence of the matter:

'Liberty and union
now and forever;'

the book on the writing-table;
the hand in the breast-pocket."

MARIANNE MOORE

"NEW" POETRY
SINCE 1912

NEW POETRY SINCE 1912

◆

Anthology of Magazine Verse (1926)

In America what is often referred to as modern poetry received marked impetus in 1912. Converted from the manner of *A Dome Of Many Coloured-Glass* (1912) to the apparently new newness of 'Imagisme' (1913), Amy Lowell became "the recognized spokesman of the Imagist group." Inaugurally arresting, however—that is to say really inaugural—Ezra Pound invented the term 'Imagisme'; and 'A Few Don'ts By An Imagist' presented by him in 1913 in the March issue of *Poetry: A Magazine of Verse*, advocated composing "in sequence of the musical phrase, not in sequence of a metronome; direct treatment of the thing, whether subjective or objective; the use of absolutely no word that does not contribute to the presentation"; and in 1914 with work of his own, appeared poems by Richard Aldington, F. S. Flint, H.D., Amy Lowell, Skipwith Cannéll, William Carlos Williams, James Joyce, John Cournos, F. M. "Hueffer", and Allan Upward.

Mr. Braithwaite felt in Imagisme, "an intensifying quality of mood," Richard Aldington felt in it "an accurate mystery," and in answer to the objection that Imagist poetry was "petty poetry, minutely small and intended to be so," May Sinclair observed that the critic "is not justified in counting lines." Of image-making power as "common to all poets," she remarked, "When Dante saw the souls of the damned falling like leaves down the banks of Acheron, it is an image, it is also imagery. It makes no difference whether he says they *are* leaves or only *like* leaves. The flying leaves are the perfect image of the damned souls. But when Sir John Suckling says his lady's feet peep in and out like mice he is only using imagery." H.D.'s 'Pines', i.e., 'Oread', which appeared first in Wyndham Lewis's *Blast* (1914), Richard Aldington's 'The Poplar', and Ezra Pound's 'The Garret' seem to one incontrovertibly illustrative of the Imagist doctrine.

In 1915 and 1916, under direction of Richard Aldington, *The Poets' Translation Series* was published by The Egoist Press, which was under the direction of Miss Harriet Shaw Weaver, and the starkness and purity of these translations is allied in one's mind with Imagism and Vorticism—Ezra Pound and certain of his Imagists being identical with certain of Wyndham Lewis's 'Vorticists'.

The "new" poetry seemed to justify itself as a more robust form of Japanese poetry—that is perhaps to say, of Chinese poetry although a specific and more lasting interest in Chinese poetry came later. In 1913, coincident with the translating into English of

'Gitanjali', Rabindranath Tagore visited the United States, was termed by our press, "The creator of a new age in literature," and W. B. Yeats wrote in *The Athenaeum*, "A whole people, a whole civilization, immeasurably strange to us, seems to have been taken up into this imagination; and yet we are not moved because of its strangeness, but because we have met our own image; as though we had walked in Rossetti's willow wood, or heard, perhaps for the first time in literature, our voice as in a dream." Felt by public and poets alike to be important, 'North of Boston' by Robert Frost, appeared in 1914, 'A Boy's Will' having been published the previous year.

The *Egoist*, *Poetry of Chicago*, and *The Little Review of Chicago*, were hospitable to "new" poetry, as was Alfred Kreymborg's *Others*. With a subsequently diverse and justifiable use of no rhyme, part rhyme, all rhyme, Alfred Kreymborg had to some, in his early practice of *vers libre* and his encouragement of the "vers libertine" as Louis Untermeyer denominates the writer of free verse—the aspect of a Cambodian devil-dancer. One recalls the emphatic work of William Carlos Williams whose book, *The Tempers* had appeared in 1913; a sliced and cylindrical, complicated yet simple use of words by Mina Loy; an enigmatically axiomatic 'Progression of the Verb "To Be"' by Walter Arensberg, and a poem by him entitled 'Ing' which corroborated the precisely perplexing verbal exactness of Gertrude Stein's *Tender Buttons*—a book which had already appeared.

ING

Walter Arensberg

Ing? Is it possible to mean ing?
Suppose
      for the termination in g
               a disoriented
               series
      of the simple fractures
               in sleep.
               Soporific
      has accordingly a value for soap
               so present to
               sew pieces.
                And p says: Peace is.
      And suppose the i
               to be big in ing
               as Beginning.
                    Then Ing is to ing
      as aloud
       accompanied by times
       and the meaning is a possibility
                      of ralsis.

    In Ezra Pound one recognized that precise
explicit "positiveness"—felt in him by Wallace Stevens—
and he was the "new" poetry's perhaps best apologist as
he reiterated in articles contributed to Miss Monroe's
magazine, his feeling that "there should be in America

the 'gloire de cénacle.'" "He is knowledge's lover," as Glenway Wescott has said, "speaking of it and to it an intimate idiom which is sometimes gibberish," and if his equivalents for that which is "dead" or foreign seem to some not always perspicuous, his contagiously enjoyable enjoyment of and his unpedantic rendering of "dead" language have done as much as have his own poems, one feels—to create an atmosphere in which poetry is likely to be written. Adelaide Crapsey's apartness and delicately differentiated footfalls, her pallor and color, were impressive. Wallace Stevens' sensory and technical virtuosity was perhaps the "new" poetry's greatest ornament and the almost imperceptibly modern, silver-chiming resonance of 'Peter Quince at the Clavier' did much to ameliorate popular displeasure. One recalls in 'Primordia', an insisted upon starkness:

> *The blunt ice flows down the Mississippi*
> *At night*

And a complexity of apprehension:

> *Compilation of the effects*
> *Of magenta blooming in the Judas-tree*
> *And of purple blooming in the eucalyptus—*

As Kenneth Jewett remarked (in *The Transatlantic Review*, April 1924) "his perfected, two-dimensional still lifes stand like rests or held chords in the progression of his complete harmony." T.S. Eliot's scrutiny of words and of behavior was apparent in his 'Portrait of a Lady'. Mr. Eliot "has not confined himself to genre nor to society portraiture," says Ezra Pound; "His

lonely men in shirt sleeves leaning out of windows

are as real as his ladies who come and go;

Talking of Michelangelo."

Writers of free verse were, for the most part, regarded as having been influenced by Laforgue, Rimbaud, and other French poets. Alfred Kreymborg, Maxwell Bodenheim, Carl Sandburg, Marsden Hartley, Muna Lee, Wallace Gould, Man Ray, Adolf Wolff, Helen Hoyt, Orrick Johns, Conrad Aiken, Amy Lowell, Evelyn Scott, Lola Ridge, Marjorie Allen Seiffert, Donald Evans, Emanuel Carnevali, Arthur Davison Ficke, and Witter Bynner, contributed to making respectable as poetry, verse which was not rhymed. In 1916, certain of these, under the names Emanuel Morgan, Anne Knish, Elijah Hay, purporting to be a new school, termed themselves 'Spectrists'. Vachel Lindsay's declamatory and in some respects unesthetic pictorialism (1915-16), pleased, displeased, and pleased the public—his originality in "trading rhymes for bread" having earlier made a good impression. Resisted and advertised, Edgar Lee

Masters' *Spoon River Anthology* (1915) seemed a technical pronunciamento.

One associates with 1921 rather than with 1913, 1915, 1916, or 1917, the morosely imaginative and graphic work of D. H. Lawrence and recalls his introversive but in mood none the less emancipated poem, 'Snake':

> *He drank enough*
> *And lifted his head, dreamily as one who has drunken,*
> *And flickered his tongue like a forked night on the air,*
> > *so black,*
> > *Seeming to lick his lips,*
> *And looked around like a god, unseeing into the air*

In 1920 and 1921, readers of new poetry noted the work of E. E. Cummings—its sleights of motion and emotion. A great deal has been made of the small "i" as used by Mr. Cummings and of certain subsidiary characteristically intentional typographic revivals and innovations on his part. While "extreme," he is, however, "only superficially modern," as has been pointed out by Dr. W.C. Blum, and truly major aspects of his work are "feeling for American speech," "rapid unfailing lyrical invention," ability to convey the sense of speed, "of change of position," "the sensations of effective effort."

Various child poets received, in 1920, the respectful attention of the public. American Indian poetry has also, at intervals, been introduced to us, as has the Negro spiritual. Leon Srabian Herald, though as yet without full command of technique, Glenway Wescott, and Yvor Winters—the one somewhat delicately Persian, the other somewhat constricted—R . Ellsworth Larsson, Harold Monro, Peter Quennell, Edith Sitwell, Osbert and Sacheverell Sitwell, have produced work which is, if not purely modern, properly within the new movement. Catholic in using either rhyme or no rhyme, certain others, not modern, yet by no means old-fashioned, manifest vigor which predominates it would seem, over newness. In Joseph Auslander, for example, we find a centaur-like and entrenched individuality of this non-conforming variety.

One recognizes in Ralph Cheever Dunning's depth and sobriety of treatment, a phase of contemporary watchfulness against ineptness. Although not especially recent, Mr. Dunning evinces, as Ezra Pound has observed, "clarity of impact," "surety," "exact termination of expression," "originality" in being superior to current fashions in verse.

Categorically "formal," as are George Dillon and Archibald MacLeish, Scofield Thayer is a new Victorian-reflective, bi-visioned, and rather wilfully unconventional. We have a mixture, apparently, of reading and of asserted detachment from reading, emotion being expressed through literal use of detail:

> *I agitate the gracile crescent*
> *Which calls itself a fern:*

And through what seems a specific reviving of incident. Tension affords strength, as is felt in certain verbally opposed natural junctures of the unexpected—"a gentle keenness," "gradual flames," "concision of a flame gone stone"—the mechanics being that of resistance.

It is perhaps beside the point to examine novel aspects of successive phases of poetic expression, inherited poetry having been at one time new, and new poetry even in its eccentricities seeming to have its counterpart in the poetry of the past in Hebrew poetry, Greek poetry, Chinese poetry. That which is weak is soon gone; that which has value does, by some strange perpetuity, live as part of the serious continuation of literature.

> *This Space for Your*
> *Thoughts*

THE OLD EXPRESSIONS ARE WITH US ALWAYS
AND THERE ARE ALWAYS OTHERS

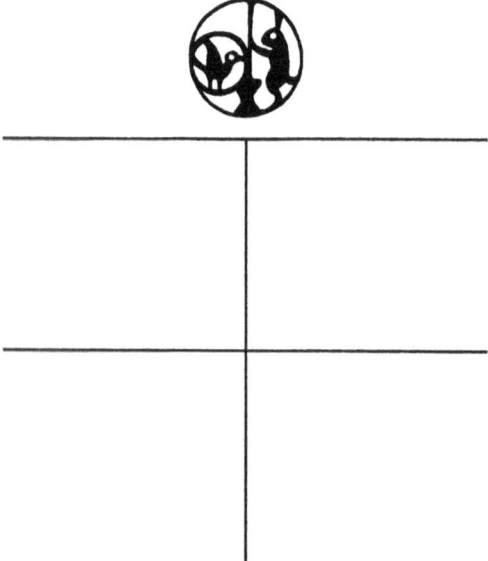

Please handle with care.